A

HENRY FORD

DISCOVER THE LIFE OF AN INVENTOR

Ann Gaines

Rourke Publishing LLC
Vero Beach, Florida 32964

www.rourkepublishing.com

PHOTO CREDITS:
©Archive Photos, The U.T.I. of Texan Cultures, Texas Department of Transportation

EDITORIAL SERVICES:
Pamela Schroeder

Library of Congress Cataloging-in-Publication Data

Gaines, Ann.
  Henry Ford / Ann Gaines
`   p. cm. — (Discover the life of an inventor)
  Includes bibliographical references and index.
  ISBN 1-58952-120-X
   1. Ford, Henry, 1863-1947—Juvenile literature. 2. Automobile industry and
trade—United States—Biography—Juvenile literature. 3. Industrialists—
United States—Biography—Juvenile literture. 4. Automobile engineersw—
United Staqtes—Biography—Juvenile literature. [1. Ford, Henry, 1863-
1947. 2. Industrialists. 3. Automobile industry and trade—Biography.] I.
Title.

TL140.F6 G35 2001
338.7'6292'092—dc21
[B]   2001019373

Printed in the USA

TABLE OF CONTENTS

HENRY FORD AND HIS IMPORTANT IDEAS

Henry Ford was an inventor. His ideas changed cars and factories. Before 1908, cars cost a lot of money. Only rich people could buy them.

Henry Ford found a way for his factory to make cars quickly. In 1908, his Ford Motor Company made a car called the Model T. Because it did not take as long to make, the Model T cost less than other cars.

American inventor Henry Ford

HENRY FORD GROWS UP

Henry Ford was born on July 30, 1863. He grew up on his parents' farm in Wayne County, Michigan. Henry loved to work on the farm machinery. He was good at fixing things and could even repair watches.

When he was 13, Henry watched a machine saw wood. A **steam engine** gave the machine its power. Henry Ford wanted to build that kind of machine, too.

The steam engine inspired Ford to make a car.

HENRY FORD GETS A START IN DETROIT

When he was 16 years old, Henry moved to Detroit. For the next few years, he worked in shops that made parts for machines. He spent his spare time building **gasoline engines**.

He married Clara Jane Bryant on April 11, 1888. In 1893 they had a son, Edsel.

In 1891 Henry began working for Thomas Edison's Illuminating Company. He became chief engineer at the power company.

Henry Ford worked for the famous inventor Thomas Edison.

MAKING CARS

At home, Henry worked on building a car. In 1896 he made a gasoline-powered car. Because it had bicycle tires, he called it the Quadricycle.

In 1903 Henry opened the Ford Motor Company. It took a long time to make a car. Henry tried to think of a way to make cars more quickly.

This picture shows Henry Ford sitting in the first car he built.

THE MODEL T ASSEMBLY LINE

In 1908 Henry Ford found his answer. He changed the way his factory made cars. Most cars were made by one team of workers who put together each part of the car. Ford's Model T **assembly line** was different. It used many teams. Each team did one job again and again.

Workers make cars on the assembly line.

The frame of the Model T was placed at the start of the assembly line. One team of workers placed the wheels on the frame. The frame and wheels then moved to another team. They added the engine, and so on down the line. Making cars this way was easy. It did not cost too much. Ford's company could sell them at low prices.

Because of its low price, many families could afford the Model T.

AMERICA'S BEST-SELLING CAR

Thanks to the assembly line, many people could afford a Model T. Thousands bought them. The Model T was America's best-selling car until 1927.

The Model T changed America. People stopped riding horses to get around. They paved old roads and made new ones. Travel became much easier.

The Model T made traveling around easier.

THE INVENTOR AND HIS
TWO LONG-LASTING INVENTIONS

Henry Ford worked on cars and other ideas until he died in 1947. Today his company remains one of the leading car makers. The Model T lasted a long time. A few Model T cars still share the road with the new Ford cars.

Henry Ford and his son Edsel stand in front of a Ford car.

Henry's assembly line is now used to make many things. Not only cars, but washing machines, televisions, toys, and even candy bars are made on assembly lines. Today Americans can learn about Henry Ford at the **Smithsonian Institution** in Washington, D.C., and at the Henry Ford Museum in Dearborn, Michigan.

IMPORTANT DATES TO REMEMBER

1863	Born in Wayne County, Michigan (July 30)
1888	Married Clara Jane Bryant
1891	Began work at Thomas Edison's Illuminating Company
1896	Made the Quadricycle
1903	Opened the Ford Motor Company
1908	Sold the first Model T Ford
1918	Half of all cars in U.S. were Model T Fords
1947	Died in Dearborn, Michigan (April 7)

GLOSSARY

assembly line (eh SEM blee LYN) — a path in a factory where something is put together

gasoline engine (GAS eh leen EN jin) — engine powered by gasoline, a colorless liquid made from oil

Smithsonian Institution (smith SOH nee un in steh TOO shen) — a famous science and technology museum in Washington, D.C.

steam engine (STEEM EN jin) — an engine that is run by steam from boiling water

INDEX

Further Reading

Coffey, Frank, and Joseph Layden. *America of Wheels, The First 100 Years: 1896-1996.* General Publishing Group, 1996.
Flammang, James M. *Cars.* Enslow, 2001.
Shaefer, Lola M. *Henry Ford.* Pebble Books, 2000.

Websites To Visit

www.umd.umich.edu/fairlane
www.hfmgv.org
www.pbs.org/wgbh/aso

About The Author

Ann Gaines is the author of many children's nonfiction books. She has also worked as a researcher in the American Civilization Program at the University of Texas.